The Year in History

Whitman Publishing, LLC

www.whitman.com

© 2012 Whitman Publishing, LLC

3101 Clairmont Rd., Suite G, Atlanta GA 30329

Correspondence concerning this book may be directed to the publisher at the address above, attention: The Year in History: 1962.

ISBN: 079483731X

Printed in China

Scan the QR code at left or visit us at www.whitman.com for a complete listing of collectibles-related books, supplies, and storage products.

Whitman®

Contents

Introduction

To say that 1962 was a landmark year would be the mother of all understatements. It was a year where we as a society watched our highest aspirations and our darkest fears become reality before our eyes. It seemed as if every day brought new announcements of the best and worst to our doorsteps. 1962 was a year that tested our resolve as a nation and as citizens of the world and showed promise of bigger and more exciting things yet to come.

Upon taking office, President John F. Kennedy pledged that the United States would put a man on the moon by the end of the decade. The Cold War between America and the Soviet Union had grown to terrifying proportions, with both sides building vast arsenals of nuclear weapons and assembling blocs of allies and client-states, raising fears that the ideological conflict between the Western democracies and the Communist apparatus would, at any moment, suddenly erupt into actual war. Add to that Soviet advancements in the space race, first with the launch of the *Sputnik* satellite and then the triumph of cosmonaut Yuri Gagarin as the first man in space, and it was clear that the American people needed a cause, an inspiration, and an awakening of their pioneer spirit.

Kennedy's commitment to the space program was just the rallying point we needed. As billions of dollars were funneled into technology and development, NASA undertook its mandate with a vengeance, and 1962 saw Americans complete the first manned orbits of Earth, launch space probes that brought back the first data from other planets, and position satellites that enabled instantaneous transmissions across the globe. By the end of the year, Kennedy's promise of a moon landing was more than a pipe dream; it was on its way.

While we kept one optimistic eye on the sky, however, the other eye strayed southward, where our worst imaginings seemed to be coming true just 90 miles off the coast of Florida. The island nation of Cuba, still smarting from President Kennedy's failed attempt to oust Premier Fidel Castro in the 1961 Bay of Pigs invasion, entered an alliance with the Soviet Union.

Intelligence reports began to come in that Cuba was not just a trade partner with the Soviets but a military ally as well, as missile installations began to pop up on the island. Suddenly America found itself faced with the prospect of a nuclear threat in its backyard. The president threw down a gauntlet and demanded the removal of the weapons, mobilizing the U.S. military to enforce his edict. The Cuban Missile Crisis proved to be the closest the world has ever come to nuclear war before or since.

At home, the civil rights movement had begun to mobilize in numbers to protest discrimination against blacks in hiring, social services, and education. Leaders like Dr. Martin Luther King Jr. staged boycotts and sit-ins to disrupt businesses they felt were hostile to blacks, and the fall of 1962 saw a showdown between the state of Mississippi and the federal government over the admission of a black student, James Meredith, to the state university. Kennedy had committed himself to support of the civil rights movement, but binding legislation to combat racial discrimination was still a long way off.

The year was not just a watershed politically. In this year Bob Dylan released his first album and began work on his second, the Beatles emerged from nightclub obscurity and began recording, and the Rolling Stones gave the first in a long career of legendary performances. Barbra Streisand made her debut on Broadway, and Ray Charles stunned the critics by releasing an album of country music that became one of the most successful records of his career.

In movie theaters, 1962 was the year that brought us some of the greatest films ever made, from the epic sweep of *Lawrence of Arabia* to the powerful statement of human dignity that was *To Kill a Mockingbird*. The film of Nabokov's controversial novel *Lolita* was released that year, and one of the most successful film franchises of all was launched as Sean Connery ordered his first martini—shaken, not stirred—as James Bond in *Dr. No.*

Filled with historic moments and bright beginnings, 1962 was a game-changing year, the effects of which are still felt to this day. We reached for the stars and came close to the end of the world. It was a momentous time to be alive.

Future comedienne and television personality Rosie O'Donnell is born in Bayside, Queens, New York on March 21.

Famous People Born in 1962

The list of celebrities born in 1962 includes some of the biggest, most bankable, and most influential figures in the world today, people who directly shape what informs and entertains the modern world. The fact that so many of them have already had long and lucrative careers at such a relatively young age is a testament to the changes that marked the 20th century. The tastemakers of the world have grown considerably younger than in decades past—fewer suits, more style.

What is interesting about the crop of celebrities born in 1962 is that many of them currently reside in the select group of "won't get out of bed for less than" stars, meaning that today they can ask for, and receive, paychecks larger than the cost of making entire movies. Granted, 1962 dollars aren't the same as current dollars, but if you had looked at an infant Tom Cruise or Jim Carrey and suggested that each of them would grow up to command salaries larger than $20 million per picture—the end profit of *Lawrence of Arabia*, the most successful picture of 1962—people would have thought you insane.

This, then, is the list of famous people born in 1962, many of whom get out of the crib every day to thrill us, entertain us, make us dance, and rock our socks off.

Comic-actor-to-be Steve Carell is born on August 16 in Concord, Massachusetts.

January 11—Kim Coles, television actress and comedian (*Living Single*)

January 13—Trace Adkins, singer (*Songs About Me*)

January 17—Jim Carrey, film actor and comedian (*The Truman Show*)

January 17—Sebastian Junger, author (*The Perfect Storm*)

January 28—Creflo Dollar, evangelist (World Changers Church International)

January 28—Sam Phillips, singer-songwriter (*A Boot and a Shoe*)

January 29—Nicholas Turturro, television actor (*NYPD Blue*)

January 30—King Abdullah II of Jordan

February 4—Clint Black, singer (*The Hard Way*)

February 5—Jennifer Jason Leigh, film actress (*Fast Times at Ridgemont High*)

February 6—Axl Rose, singer (Guns N' Roses)

February 7—Garth Brooks, singer (*No Fences*)

February 7—Eddie Izzard, film and television actor and comedian (*Dressed to Kill*)

February 11—Sheryl Crow, singer-songwriter (*Tuesday Night Music Club*)

February 17—Lou Diamond Phillips, actor (*La Bamba*)

February 21—Chuck Palahniuk, author (*Fight Club*)

February 21—David Foster Wallace, author (*Infinite Jest*)

February 22—Steve Irwin, naturalist and television host (*The Crocodile Hunter*; d. 2006)

February 24—Michelle Shocked, singer-songwriter (*Short Sharp Shocked*)

February 27—Adam Baldwin, film and television actor (*Firefly*)

March 2—Jon Bon Jovi, singer (Bon Jovi)

March 3—Jackie Joyner-Kersee, Olympic gold medalist (heptathlon)

March 3—Herschel Walker, football running back and Heisman Trophy winner

March 7—Taylor Dayne, singer (*Tell It to My Heart*)

March 10—Jasmine Guy, stage and television actress (*A Different World*)

March 12—Darryl Strawberry, baseball right fielder (New York Yankees)

March 21—Matthew Broderick, stage and film actor (*Ferris Bueller's Day Off*)

March 21—Rosie O'Donnell, comedienne and talk-show host (*The View*)

March 24—Star Jones, talk-show host (*The View*)

March 25—Marcia Cross, television actress (*Desperate Housewives*)

March 29—Billy Beane, baseball general manager (Oakland A's)

March 30—MC Hammer, hip-hop artist (*Please Hammer Don't Hurt 'Em*)

April 3—Mike Ness, singer (Social Distortion)

April 8—Izzy Stradlin, guitarist (Guns N' Roses)

April 18—Jeff Dunham, ventriloquist and comedian (*Jeff Dunham: Spark of Insanity*)

April 19—Al Unser Jr., NASCAR driver (Indianapolis 500 winner)

Born on November 11 in Roswell, New Mexico, Demi Guynes would grow up to be actress Demi Moore.

May 7—Robbie Knievel, professional daredevil (son of Evel Knievel)

May 10—David Fincher, film director *(Se7en)*

May 12—Emilio Estevez, film actor *(The Breakfast Club)*

May 14—Ian Astbury, singer (The Cult)

May 14—Danny Huston, film actor and director (son of John Huston)

May 17—Craig Ferguson, comedian and talk-show host *(The Late Late Show with Craig Ferguson)*

May 26—Genie Francis, television actress *(General Hospital)*

May 26—Bobcat Goldthwait, film actor and comedian *(Shakes the Clown)*

May 28—Roland Gift, singer (Fine Young Cannibals)

May 31—Corey Hart, singer ("Sunglasses at Night")

June 8—Nick Rhodes, keyboardist (Duran Duran)

June 10—Gina Gershon, film actress *(Bound)*

June 13—Ally Sheedy, film actress *(The Breakfast Club)*

June 15—Thomas Mikal Ford, television actor *(Martin)*

June 19—Paula Abdul, singer and choreographer *(American Idol)*

July 3—Tom Cruise, film actor *(Rain Man)*

July 8—Joan Osborne, singer-songwriter *(Relish)*

July 13—Tom Kenny, comedian and voice actor *(Spongebob Squarepants)*

July 19—Anthony Edwards, film and television actor *(ER)*

July 21—Rob Morrow, television actor *(Northern Exposure)*

July 22—Steve Albini, musician and producer (Nirvana, Cheap Trick)

July 23—Eriq LaSalle, television actor *(ER)*

July 30—Alton Brown, chef and television host *(Good Eats)*

July 31—Fatboy Slim, musician *(Halfway Between the Gutter and the Stars)*

July 31—Wesley Snipes, film actor *(Blade)*

August 4—Roger Clemens, baseball pitcher (New York Yankees)

August 5—Patrick Ewing, basketball center (New York Knicks)

August 6—Michelle Yeoh, film actress *(Crouching Tiger, Hidden Dragon)*

August 15—Tom Colicchio, chef and television host *(Top Chef)*

August 16—Steve Carell, film and television actor *(The Office)*

August 16—James Marsters, television actor *(Buffy the Vampire Slayer)*

August 16—John Schnatter, entrepreneur (founder of Papa John's Pizza)

August 18—Felipe Calderon, President of Mexico

August 24—Craig Kilborn, television host *(ESPN SportsCenter)*

September 6—Elizabeth Vargas, television journalist *(ABC Evening News)*

September 11—Kristy McNichol, film and television actress *(Little Darlings)*

September 17—Baz Luhrmann, film director *(Moulin Rouge)*

September 19—Cheri Oteri, television actress and comedian *(Saturday Night Live)*

Jon Stewart, future political satirist and television host, is born in New York City on November 28.

September 24—Nia Vardalos, film actress and playwright *(My Big Fat Greek Wedding)*

September 25—Aida Turturro, film and television actress *(The Sopranos)*

September 26—Melissa Sue Anderson, television actress *(Little House on the Prairie)*

October 3—Tommy Lee, drummer (Mötley Crüe)

October 11—Joan Cusack, film actress and comedienne *(Grosse Point Blank)*

October 13—Kelly Preston, film actress *(Mischief)*

October 13—Jerry Rice, football wide receiver (San Francisco 49ers)

October 16—Manute Bol, basketball center (Philadelphia 76ers)

October 16—Flea (b. Michael Balzary), musician (Red Hot Chili Peppers)

October 17—Mike Judge, film and television director *(Office Space)*

October 18—Vincent Spano, film actor *(Baby, It's You)*

October 19—Tracy Chevalier, author *(The Girl With a Pearl Earring)*

October 19—Evander Holyfield, boxer (heavyweight champ)

October 22—Bob Odenkirk, television actor and comedian *(Mr. Show)*

October 26—Cary Elwes, film actor *(The Princess Bride)*

October 28—Mark Haddon, author *(The Curious Case of the Dog in the Night-Time)*

October 28—Daphne Zuniga, film and television actress *(Melrose Place)*

November 1—Anthony Kiedis, singer (Red Hot Chili Peppers)

November 4—Jeff Probst, television host *(Survivor)*

November 11—Demi Moore, film actress *(St. Elmo's Fire)*

November 12—Naomi Wolf, author *(The Beauty Myth)*

November 14—Laura San Giacomo, film and television actress *(Just Shoot Me)*

November 14—Harland Williams, film actor and comedian *(Rocket Man)*

November 19—Jodie Foster, film actress and director *(The Silence of the Lambs)*

November 27—Victoria Gotti, ex-wife of mobster John Gotti

November 28—Jon Stewart, comedian and television host *(The Daily Show with Jon Stewart)*

November 29—Andrew McCarthy, film actor *(Pretty in Pink)*

November 30—Bo Jackson, football and baseball player and Heisman Trophy winner

December 6—Janine Turner, film and television actress *(Northern Exposure)*

December 9—Felicity Huffman, film and television actress *(Desperate Housewives)*

December 12—Tracy Austin, tennis player and U.S. Open champion

December 16—William "The Refrigerator" Perry, football defensive tackle (Chicago Bears)

December 22—Ralph Fiennes, film actor *(The English Patient)*

December 24—Kate Spade, fashion designer

LONG DISTANCE CALLS

To reach the Long Distance operator **Dial Operator**

types of calls

STATION-TO-STATION

Call station-to-station if you will talk with anyone who answers. Rates are lower than person-to-person. Charging begins when the called telephone answers.

PERSON-TO-PERSON

Call person-to-person when you must talk to a particular person or extension telephone. Rates are higher than station-to-station. Charging begins when the called person or extension answers.

COLLECT

Most calls can be made "collect" if the person you are calling agrees to pay the charge. If you want the call made collect, please be sure to tell the operator when you give her the call.

MOBILE AND MARINE SERVICE

You can make local and Long Distance calls to automobiles, trucks and boats equipped with mobile telephone service. Ask Long Distance for the mobile service operator, or the marine operator.

CONFERENCE

You can talk with several people in different places at the same time. Tell the Long Distance operator you wish to make a conference call.

how to make calls

PLACING CALLS WITH OPERATOR

When you place your Long Distance calls with the operator, give her the Area Code and the telephone number. *If you do not know the Area Code, give* the name of the town and state. *If you do not know the telephone number*, give the name and address and tell the operator whether it is a station or person call.

Give your own telephone number only when the operator asks for it. Giving it to her *before* she's ready to receive it may delay the handling of your call.

OVERSEAS CALL
(Including Alaska and Hawaii)

Calls to practically all the world's telephones can be made from your telephone. Tell the Long Distance operator you wish to place an overseas call and give her the name of the overseas point you are calling.

Some typical weekday rates for a 3-minute call (excluding Federal Excise Tax)

ARGENTINA	BERMUDA	$7.50
AUSTRALIA	PANAMA	7.50
BRITISH ISLES $12.00	PUERTO RICO	6.50
ITALY	VIRGIN IS.	
JAPAN		
PHILIPPINE IS.	HAWAII	7.50

ALASKA { Anchorage $8.25 Juneau $8.25
         { Fairbanks 8.25 Nome   9.00

Reduced rates apply on calls to many countries during certain night hours and on Sundays.

LONG DISTANCE RATES from WICHITA FALLS

These typical rates are for the first 3 minutes and *do not include the* **Federal Excise Tax.** Rates are lower every night after 6 and all day Sunday, Thanksgiving, Christmas and New Year's Day. Time at the calling point governs the application of these rates. For rates to other points, dial the Long Distance operator.

	Station-to-Station Week-days	Station-to-Station Nights & Sun.	Person-to-Person Week-days	Person-to-Person Nights & Sun.		Station-to-Station Week-days	Station-to-Station Nights & Sun.	Person-to-Person Week-days	Person-to-Person Nights & Sun.		Station-to-Station Week-days	Station-to-Station Nights & Sun.	Person-to-Person Week-days
Abilene	$ .75	$ .65	$1.20	$1.10	Fayetteville, Ark.	$ .95	$ .70	$1.35	$1.10	N. Y. City, N. Y.	$1.80	$1.40	$2.85
Amarillo	.95	.80	1.50	1.35	Fort Worth	.70	.60	1.10	1.00	Nocona	.45	.45	.70
Austin	1.05	.90	1.70	1.55	Gainesville	.60	.50	.95	.85	Paris	.85	.70	1.35
Bartlesville, Okla.	.85	.65	1.20	1.00	Graham	.55	.50	.90	.85	Plainview	.90	.75	1.45
Birmingham, Ala.	1.40	1.10	1.95	1.65	Henderson	1.05	.90	1.70	1.55	Quanah	.60	.50	.95
Bowie	.45	.45	.70	.70	Houston	1.20	1.00	1.90	1.70	St. Louis, Mo.	1.35	1.05	1.90
Breckenridge	.60	.50	.95	.85	Jacksboro	.50	.50	.80	.80	San Antonio	1.15	1.00	1.85
Canyon	.95	.80	1.50	1.35	Kansas City, Mo.	1.15	.85	1.60	1.30	San Francisco, Cal.	1.80	1.40	2.85
Childress													.50 .80
Cisco													.60 1.10
Colorado City													.40 2.85
Dallas													.60 1.10
Decatur													.70 1.35
Denison													.80 1.50
Denton													.50 .80
Denver, Colo.	1.30	1.00	1.80	1.50	Montgomery, Ala.	1.45	1.15	2.10	1.80	Waco	.90	.75	1.45
Electra	.30	.30	.50	.50	New Orleans, La.	1.35	1.05	1.90	1.60	Weatherford	.65	.55	1.05

Copyright 1962 by the Southwestern Bell Telephone Company.

The **Cost** of **Living** in
1962

I t's always an eye-opener when we look back at the prices for consumer goods and see how relatively little the things we purchased seemed to cost. We say "seemed to" because we're looking at it from the perspective of people earning current wages and paying current prices. For what we were earning at the time, some of the prices we paid were shocking. On the other hand, the value of what we paid for in 1962 was, in many ways, much higher. Portions were larger. That gallon of gas came with an attendant who pumped it for you. Technologies we take for granted now were new back then.

The American economy had benefited from 17 years of the post–World War II boom that created new industries and new jobs, made the ownership of homes and cars affordable to many, and saw the rise of the suburbs. The economic picture of 1962, however, was not as rosy at it appears. Unemployment was high, particularly among minorities, and the country was struggling with the imminent threat of widespread inflation. Among the other tasks on its plate, the Kennedy administration was embroiled in a fierce battle with Congress over a mounting national debt.

In other words, though the numbers were smaller, the economics of 1962 were pretty much business as usual!

THE EL RANCHO   Designed for Comfort

This home is a Modern Beauty. We have included siding where stone is shown on front wall. If you plan to use stone, allowance will be quoted for omission of siding. Write for specifications.

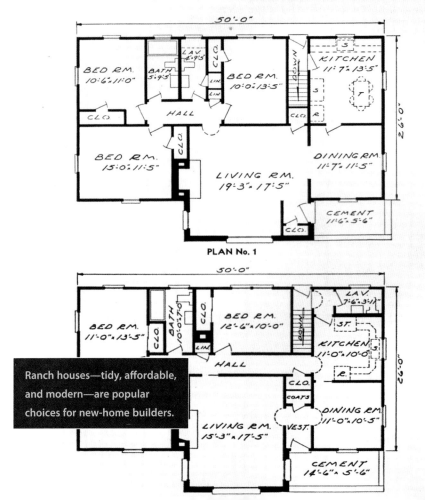

50'-0"

BED RM.
10'-6"x11'-0"

BATH
5'-9"

LAV.
4'-9"

BED RM.
10'-0"x13'-5"

KITCHEN
11'-7"x13'-5"

CLO.

HALL

BED RM.
15'-0"x11'-5"

LIVING RM.
19'-3"x17'-5"

DINING RM.
11'-7"x11'-5"

CEMENT
11'-6"x5'-6"

26'-0"

PLAN No. 1

50'-0"

BED RM.
11'-0"x13'-5"

BATH
10'-0"x7'-0"

BED RM.
12'-6"x10'-0"

LAV.
7'-6"x3'-11"

ST.

KITCHEN
11'-0"x10'-0"

HALL

CLO.

COATS

LIVING RM.
15'-3"x17'-5"

VEST.

DINING RM.
11'-0"x10'-5"

CEMENT
14'-6"x5'-6"

26'-0"

Ranch houses—tidy, affordable, and modern—are popular choices for new-home builders.

Statistics about American life in 1962:

The average American's yearly **income** was $5,556.

The minimum **wage** was $1.25 per hour.

Median income **tax** was 20%.

The annual rate of **inflation** in the United States was 1.20%.

At the end of the year, the **Dow Jones** Industrial Average was 652.

The average cost of a new **house** was $13,750.

The average monthly **rent** was $110.

Cars, household goods, and appliances:

The price of a new car: $2,500 to $3,000

Gallon of gas: 30 cents

Color television set: $400

Tape recorder: $98

Transistor radio: $40

Record player: $40

Record album: $3

45-rpm single: 50 cents

Refrigerator: $500

Electric sewing machine: $49.95

Electric can opener: $9

Hoover vacuum cleaner: $49

Desk and chair set: $40

Drop-leaf table: $18.95

Wool blanket: $16.95

Springfield rifle: $49

Groceries:

Pound of ground beef: 35 cents

Pound of round steak: $1.07

Pound of pork chops: 90 cents

Pound of bacon: 70 cents

1/2 gallon of milk: 52 cents

Loaf of bread: 20 cents

Dozen eggs: 54 cents

Pound of butter: 75 cents

Pound of margarine: 28 cents

6-lb. bag of flour: 57 cents

5-lb. bag of sugar: 59 cents

10-lb. bag of potatoes: 63 cents

Passenger cars average around 22 miles per gallon—surprising, considering that a gallon of gas costs only about 30 cents.

10-oz. can of tomatoes: 16 cents
Pound of coffee: 71 cents
18-oz. box of corn flakes: 27 cents
Pound box of Oreo cookies: 49 cents

Clothing:

Pair of tennis shoes: $5
Pair of loafers: $3
Pair of men's oxfords: $12
Pair of ladies' pumps: $6
Gabardine bomber jacket: $11
Corduroy shirt: $4
Pair of nylons: $1.15
Fashionable handbag: $6

Entertainment and dining out:

Fast-food hamburger: 20 cents
French fries: 20 cents
Small milkshake: 25 cents
Ice cream bar: 15 cents
Small cup of coffee: 12 cents
Movie ticket: 50 cents
Bag of popcorn: 20 cents
Soft drink: 10 cents
Candy bar: 5 cents
Pack of chewing gum: 5 cents

Toys:

Tricycle: $9.95
Scooter: $4.95
Roller skates: $36.95
Comic book: 12 cents

Other common purchases:

Pay phone call: 10 cents
First-class postage: 4 cents
Daily newspaper: 10 cents
Pack of king-size cigarettes: 25 cents
Pack of 100s cigarettes: 35 cents
Doctor's office visit: $5

A defining moment of a tense year: President Kennedy authorizes the naval blockade of Cuba, October 23, 1962.

Day-by-Day Calendar **of**

1962

It's a function of memory that we recall some extraordinary events that immediately affect us and submerge others. We are barraged from all sides by information and can only do so much with it, so we often forget that important and significant things are happening around us every day. A look back at the events of 1962 reveals that every single day brought something of note, sometimes trivial and sometimes earth-shattering, that impacted the world and helped to shape the future.

Following is a list of events, triumphs, and passages from the worlds of news, sports, and entertainment, drawn from newspapers, radio and television broadcasts, encyclopedia sources, and historical archives. Together they form a journal tracking the progress of the U.S. and the world as we navigated through uncertain and often turbulent waters.

JANUARY 1

The United States Navy SEALs (SEa, Air, and Land teams) are activated in response to escalating unrest in Southeast Asia. Two elite teams, specializing in demolitions and unconventional warfare, are assigned to the Pacific and Atlantic fleets.

JANUARY 2

President John F. Kennedy receives a commendation from the NAACP for his "personal role" in advancing civil rights.

JANUARY 3

The Cuban prime minister is excommunicated from the Catholic Church by Pope John XXIII, who cites multiple violations of the Code of Canon Law.

JANUARY 4

New York City introduces the first subway train that operates without onboard crew.

JANUARY 5

The first known recording of the Beatles, backing English pop star Tony Sheridan as "The Beat Brothers," is released on the Polydor label.

JANUARY 6

The *Los Angeles Mirror-News* newspaper publishes its final issue.

JANUARY 7

A bomb destroys the Paris apartment of existentialist philosopher and author Jean-Paul Sartre, who is away from home at the time.

JANUARY 8

The *Mona Lisa* is exhibited for the first time in the United States, at the National Gallery of Art in Washington, D.C.

JANUARY 9

Cuba enters a trade agreement with the Soviet Union.

JANUARY 10

An explosion in a coal mine near Carterville, Illinois, claims the lives of 11 miners.

JANUARY 11

Anti-apartheid leader Nelson Mandela leaves South Africa illegally to begin a six-month speaking tour of the continent. He is arrested upon his return.

JANUARY 12

The United States carries out its first covert combat operation in Vietnam, called "Operation Chopper."

JANUARY 13

TV comedian Ernie Kovacs is killed in an automobile crash in Los Angeles, California.

JANUARY 14

The Western Conference pulls off a last-minute upset to win the National Football League Pro Bowl 31–30 in Los Angeles.

JANUARY 15

Chubby Checker's "The Twist" is the number one pop single in America.

JANUARY 16

Principal shooting begins on *Dr. No,* the first film in the
long-running James Bond movie franchise.

In September, McDonald's files a trademark for a single arch, like this one in Pine Bluff,
Arkansas. The famous "golden arches" won't appear until 1968.

JANUARY 17

Ten former contestants, including prominent professor
Charles Van Doren, plead guilty to charges of perjury during
a Congressional investigation of cheating on TV game shows.

JANUARY 18

The American military begins using defoliant on the dense jungle
growth of Vietnam to eliminate Viet Cong guerilla cover.

JANUARY 19

KGB agents identify and arrest Colonel Oleg Penkovsky for
turning over secret information to British intelligence pertaining
to the placement of Soviet nuclear missiles in Cuba. This information
will contribute to the Cuban Missile Crisis later in the year.

JANUARY 20

Robinson Jeffers, influential poet and environmental activist,
dies in Carmel, California, at age 75.

JANUARY 21

At a meeting of the Organization of American States in Uruguay, the United States agrees to provide aid to Haiti in exchange for the nation's support of the American embargo of Cuba.

JANUARY 22

The Organization of American States suspends Cuba's membership.

JANUARY 23

Jackie Robinson, the first black player in Major League Baseball, is inducted into the Baseball Hall of Fame.

JANUARY 24

Brian Epstein becomes the Beatles' manager in a verbal agreement that gives him 25 percent of the band's earnings.

JANUARY 25

Montana governor Donald G. Nutter is killed in a plane crash along with five others.

JANUARY 26

NASA launches *Ranger 3,* a space probe designed to land on the moon. It is later announced that the rocket's trajectory has erred and missed the moon by more than 22,000 miles.

JANUARY 27

The planned spaceflight of *Friendship 7* is scrubbed 20 minutes before scheduled liftoff due to technical difficulties and inclement weather. Astronaut John Glenn's orbit of Earth is postponed.

JANUARY 28

The last streetcar in Washington, D.C., is retired.

JANUARY 29

The automobile industry announces that the forward turn signals on all American cars will now be amber-colored, to distinguish them from the headlights.

JANUARY 30

Two members of the famed aerialist troupe the Flying Wallendas die in a mishap while performing their signature seven-person pyramid during a performance in Detroit.

JANUARY 31

Joey Dee and the Starliters hit number one on the charts with "Peppermint Twist."

FEBRUARY 1

President Kennedy calls for job training and child care to become integral components of federal welfare programs.

On January 9, the president of Cuba, Fidel Castro (shown here at an earlier UN General Assembly), enters his country into a trade agreement with the Soviet Union.

FEBRUARY 2

The U.S. Air Force suffers its first casualties in Vietnam as a defoliant-spraying plane goes down in the jungle. It is undetermined whether the plane was shot down.

FEBRUARY 3

The United States announces a unilateral embargo against trade and travel between the U.S. and Cuba in protest against Fidel Castro's Soviet-backed government.

FEBRUARY 4

St. Jude's Children's Hospital, founded by comedian Danny Thomas and committed to providing free care for needy children, opens.

FEBRUARY 5

A solar eclipse occurs along with a conjunction of the five planets visible to the naked eye (Mercury, Venus, Mars, Jupiter, and Saturn) as well as the moon, the first such lining-up to occur since 1821.

FEBRUARY 6

The city of Memphis, Tennessee, desegregates lunch counters after widespread civil rights protests and sit-ins.

FEBRUARY 7

The U.S. air force issues a public statement that "Project Blue Book," its task force investigating UFO claims, has failed to find any evidence of extraterrestrial visitations on Earth.

FEBRUARY 8

The United Kingdom agrees to allow American nuclear weapons testing on Christmas Island, a British possession in the Pacific Ocean.

FEBRUARY 9

The Taiwan Stock Exchange opens.

FEBRUARY 10

Francis Gary Powers, pilot of an American U-2 spy plane shot down over the Soviet Union in 1960, is released to U.S. intelligence agents in Berlin in exchange for Soviet agent Rudolf Abel.

FEBRUARY 11

June Carter becomes a regular part of country singer Johnny Cash's touring ensemble. The two would marry in 1968.

FEBRUARY 12

Gene Chandler's "Duke of Earl" tops the pop charts.

FEBRUARY 13

Sergeants 3, a remake of *Gunga Din,* is the number one movie in America.

FEBRUARY 14

First Lady Jacqueline Kennedy hosts a televised tour of the White House. It is the most widely viewed TV program ever, watched by 75% of the American viewing public.

FEBRUARY 15

June Marina Oswald, daughter of future Kennedy assassin Lee Harvey Oswald, is born in Minsk, USSR.

FEBRUARY 16

President Kennedy issues executive orders calling for "emergency preparedness" measures to be put in place in the event that the administration declares martial law.

FEBRUARY 17

Actress Elizabeth Taylor attempts suicide by prescription-drug overdose during the filming of *Cleopatra* after a reported falling-out with both her husband Eddie Fisher and her costar Richard Burton.

A U.S. Air Force UC-123B sprays defoliant over a patch of Vietnamese jungle.

FEBRUARY 18

Hotel and gambling magnate Baron Long, owner of the Agua Caliente Racetrack and a casino hotel of the same name, dies at age 78.

FEBRUARY 19

Georgios Papanikolaou, inventor of the Babeş-Papanicolaou test or "Pap smear," which facilitates early detection of uterine and cervical cancer, dies at the age of 78.

FEBRUARY 20

Astronaut John Glenn becomes the first American in orbit as his capsule, *Friendship 7*, circles Earth three times in four hours, 55 minutes.

FEBRUARY 21

The United States launches its first Samos-F satellite, designed for reconnaissance on the Soviet Union, into orbit.

FEBRUARY 22

"A Little Bitty Tear" by Burl Ives tops the easy-listening charts.

FEBRUARY 23

Meeting with President Kennedy after returning from orbit, John Glenn reveals that the heat shield on his capsule had begun to break up during re-entry, a potentially fatal malfunction.

FEBRUARY 24

The U.S. government transmits its first telecommunications signal via the *Echo I* satellite.

FEBRUARY 25

Kenny Ball and his Jazzmen have a number one easy-listening hit with "Midnight in Moscow."

FEBRUARY 26

Arthur L. Kopit's absurdist play *Oh Dad, Poor Dad, Mama's Hung You in the Closet and I'm Feelin' So Sad: A Pseudoclassical Tragifarce in a Bastard French Tradition* opens in New York. The play, about an overprotective mother, her neurotic son, the corpse of her husband, and her man-eating plant, would move to Broadway, win several awards, and become a major motion picture in 1967.

FEBRUARY 27

FBI director J. Edgar Hoover provides attorney general Robert F. Kennedy, brother of the president, with information of secret communications between the president and socialite Judith Exner. It is widely believed that Kennedy had planned to remove Hoover as director up until that meeting.

FEBRUARY 28

A U.S. air force base in Cigli, Turkey, armed with 15 nuclear missiles within striking range of the Soviet Union, goes operational. The presence of these missiles will be a point of contention during the Cuban Missile Crisis.

MARCH 1

The first K-Mart store opens in Garden City, Michigan.

MARCH 2

Wilt Chamberlain sets an as-yet unbroken NBA record by scoring 100 points in a single game, leading his Philadelphia Warriors to victory over the New York Knickerbockers.

MARCH 3

The University of Wisconsin men's basketball team, which has never beaten a number-one-ranked team, pulls off the upset of the season by defeating previously unbeaten Ohio State 86–67.

MARCH 4

Representatives of 18 nations, including the nuclear powers France, Great Britain, the Soviet Union, and the United States, meet in Geneva, Switzerland, to conduct disarmament talks.

MARCH 5

Bruce Cahannel has the number one pop single in America with "Hey Baby."

Charles "Lucky" Luciano, the father of modern organized crime, dies of a heart attack on January 26 at Naples International Airport.

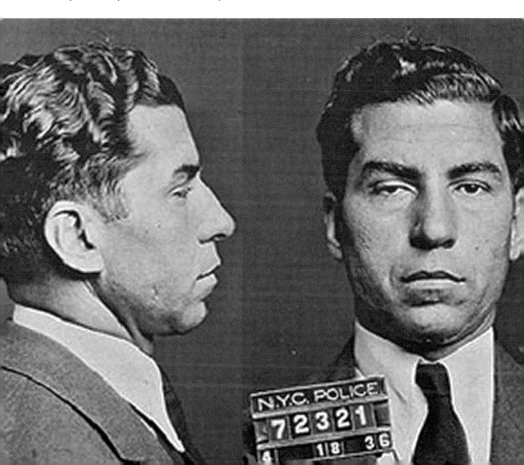

MARCH 6

The "Ash Wednesday Storm" hits the coast of North Carolina and batters the East Coast for three days, with a death toll of 40 and damage in excess of half a billion dollars. Destructive winds and monstrously high tides make it one of the worst storms ever to hit the United States.

MARCH 7

The United States launches the first of nine orbiting solar observatory satellites, designed to measure solar radiation.

MARCH 8

Thalidomide, a sedative prescribed to treat morning sickness in expectant mothers, is withdrawn from the market after it is revealed to be responsible for widespread birth defects.

MARCH 9

The Premature Burial, based on a story by Edgar Allan Poe and directed by Roger Corman, is the top-grossing film in the United States.

MARCH 10

"Misery Loves Company" by Porter Wagoner tops the country charts.

MARCH 11

First Lady Jacqueline Kennedy has a 33-minute audience with Pope John XXIII, one of the longest visits this papacy has granted.

MARCH 12

In the wake of the American embargo, Cuba begins food rationing.

MARCH 13

General L.L. Lemnitzer, chairman of the Joint Chiefs of Staff, presents defense secretary Robert McNamara with a proposed plan to stage "terrorist acts" within the United States that can be blamed on Cuba, in order to drum up support for an invasion there. McNamara rejects the plan on the spot.

MARCH 14

Edward M. Kennedy, brother of the president, announces his candidacy for senator from Massachusetts, three weeks past turning the required age of 30. He would win the seat and hold it for the next 37 years.

MARCH 15

President Kennedy asks Congress to pass a "Consumer Bill of Rights" that will strengthen the federal government's role in consumer protection and product regulation.

MARCH 16

The USSR launches the first *Kosmos* satellite into orbit, to monitor the ionosphere and to test its payload rocket.

MARCH 17

Wilhelm Blaschke, German mathematician and pioneer in the field of classical geometry, dies at age 76.

MARCH 18

Sheb Woolley's "That's My Pa" is the number one country hit in America.

MARCH 19

State Fair, starring Pat Boone, is the top movie in America.

MARCH 20

C. Wright Mills, an influential sociologist whose books *The Power Elite* and *The Sociological Imagination* had a profound impact on modern thought about class structure and capitalism in American society, dies in West Nyack, New York, at age 45.

MARCH 21

President Kennedy announces that he and Soviet premier Nikita Khrushchev have agreed to initiate a future joint space-exploration venture. This will come to fruition with the *Apollo-Soyuz* mission of 1975.

William Bruce Rose Jr. is born on Feb. 6 in Lafayette, Indiana. When he grows up, he will be known as Axl Rose, vocalist for Guns N' Roses.

MARCH 22

Pakistani president Mohammed Ayub Khan presents First Lady Jacqueline Kennedy with a bay gelding named Sardar ("chief" in Arabic) as a state gift.

MARCH 23

Barbra Streisand receives a rave review from *The New York Times* for her debut performance on Broadway in *I Can Get It for You Wholesale*.

MARCH 24

At Madison Square Garden, Emile Griffith knocks our Benny "The Kid" Paret in the 12th round to take the world welterweight boxing title. Paret dies ten days later from head injuries he received during the bout.

MARCH 25

"Don't Break the Heart That Loves You" becomes a number one hit for Connie Francis on both the pop and easy-listening charts.

MARCH 26

The U.S. Supreme Court rules that federal courts may decide the constitutionality of state reapportionment, thus providing a check against gerrymandering by state legislatures.

MARCH 27

Unusually powerful solar flares cause the Northern
Lights to appear over Chicago, Illinois.

MARCH 28

Deciding on a discrimination lawsuit, a Louisiana district court rules that
Tulane University is a public institution and must admit black students.

MARCH 29

Jack Paar makes his final appearance as host of *The Tonight Show*.

MARCH 30

Martin Luther King Jr. sends a telegram to President Kennedy urging him
to consider judges William Hastie and Thurgood Marshall for an open
Supreme Court appointment. Byron White receives the appointment, but
Marshall would be appointed in 1967 by Kennedy's successor, Lyndon Johnson.

MARCH 31

"She's Got You" by Patsy Cline is the number
one country single in the United States.

APRIL 1

"Johnny Angel" by Shelley Fabares tops the pop charts.

APRIL 2

The top-grossing film in America is *Sweet Bird of Youth,* an adaptation of the Tennessee Williams play of the same name. It stars Paul Newman and Geraldine Page.

APRIL 3

Jawaharlal Nehru becomes prime minister of India.

APRIL 4

The city of Birmingham, Alabama, suspends its program of supplying surplus food to the poor in retaliation for African American boycotts of downtown businesses.

APRIL 5

Herb Gardner's *A Thousand Clowns* opens on Broadway. It would go on to win the Tony Award for Best Play in 1963.

APRIL 6

New York Philharmonic conductor Leonard Bernstein creates
a stir when he issues a disclaimer before a performance by
the notoriously volatile but brilliant pianist Glenn Gould.
Bernstein's public remark is credited by many with
causing Gould's early retirement from performing.

Mrs. John F. Kennedy, in her first official White House photo, is well on her way to being an
American fashion icon.

APRIL 7

Soviet Premier Nikita Khrushchev warns the United States
not to violate a nuclear weapons test ban treaty.

APRIL 8

Juan Belmonte Garcia, considered the greatest
matador of all time, dies in Spain at age 70.

APRIL 9

Golfer Arnold Palmer wins the Masters Tournament in
Augusta, Georgia, for the third time after defeating Gary Player
and Dow Finsterwald in the tournament's first three-way playoff.

APRIL 10

Dodger Stadium opens. The home of the Los Angeles Dodgers,
it is also the home field of the Los Angeles Angels until 1965.

APRIL 11

The New York Mets (Metropolitans) play their first game as a baseball franchise.

APRIL 12

Byron White is sworn in as a U.S. Supreme Court justice.

APRIL 13

The Beatles begin their "residency" at the Star Club in Hamburg,
Germany, playing every night for the next seven weeks.

APRIL 14

Packy, the first baby elephant conceived and birthed
in a United States zoo, is born in Portland, Oregon.

APRIL 15

"Good Luck Charm" by Elvis Presley is the number one pop single in America.

APRIL 16

Walter Cronkite, who will become known as "the most
trusted man in America," becomes anchor of the
CBS Evening News, a job he will hold for the next 19 years.

APRIL 17

Experiment in Terror, starring Glenn Ford and Lee Remick, is the number one film in the country.

APRIL 18

The Boston Celtics defeat the Los Angeles Lakers 110–107 in overtime in the seventh and deciding game of the NBA Finals.

APRIL 19

NASA announces the Project Gemini program.

APRIL 20

Under the supervision of professors Timothy Leary and Richard Alpert, Harvard psychologist Walter Pahnke conducts the "Good Friday experiment," administering doses of the psychedelic drug psilocybin to theology students to determine whether hallucinogens can trigger religious experiences.

APRIL 21

In Seattle, Washington, the Century 21 Exposition World's Fair opens to the public. With a focus on the space race and futurism, the fair features Seattle's landmark Space Needle as its centerpiece.

APRIL 22

The Toronto Maple Leafs win the Stanley Cup, defeating the Black Hawks
in Chicago in the sixth game of the best-of-seven playoffs.

Tetra Classic Aseptic packages hold everything from ice cream to orange juice.
The rectangular box is still a year from the market.

APRIL 23

Follow That Dream, starring Elvis Presley, is the top-grossing film in America.

APRIL 24

Engineers at MIT send a signal via satellite from Massachusetts to California.

APRIL 25

The United States begins nuclear weapons testing on Christmas Island in the Pacific in response to the Soviet Union's breach of a moratorium on the practice.

APRIL 26

American space probe *Ranger 4* reaches the moon, crash-landing on the dark side.

APRIL 27

Police officers engage in a clash with members of the Nation of Islam in a Los Angeles mosque, leaving several people dead or injured. This event is thought by many to be a cause of Malcolm X's later separation from the organization and a contributing factor to the Watts riots of 1965.

APRIL 28

"Charlie's Shoes" by Billy Walker tops the country charts.

APRIL 29

The Shirelles have a number one single with "Soldier Boy."

APRIL 30

The number one film in America is *The Man Who Shot Liberty Valance,* starring Jimmy Stewart and John Wayne.

MAY 1

The first Target department store opens in Roseville, Minnesota.

MAY 2

East Germany and Yugoslavia display newly acquired Soviet military hardware such as tanks and missiles, revealing that the Soviet Union is now supplying its satellite states with weapons.

MAY 3

Two commuter trains and a freight train collide just outside Tokyo, killing 160 and injuring more than 400.

MAY 4

A. Philip Randolph, president of the Negro American Labor Council, requests a conference with President Kennedy to address the unemployment rate among minorities.

MAY 5

Decidedly, an American Thoroughbred, wins the Kentucky Derby.

MAY 6

The USS *Ethan Allen,* a Navy submarine in the Pacific, launches a Polaris nuclear missile in a live-fire test, the only such firing before or since. The test is successful, the missile yielding 600 kilotons at an altitude of 11,000 feet.

MAY 7

President Kennedy warns the United Auto Workers to exercise wage restraints to avoid inflation.

MAY 8

Stephen Sondheim's musical *A Funny Thing Happened on the Way to the Forum* opens at the Alvin Theatre in New York, where it will run for over 900 performances.

Television is the latest thing, but it's at a disadvantage with the radio transmission from the *Friendship 7*. As astronaut John Glenn speaks, TVs display a technical-looking panel with the words "Glenn's Voice" printed above it.

MAY 9

Scientists at the Massachusetts Institute of Technology (MIT) fire
a telescope-mounted laser beam at the moon to measure distance.
The beam strikes the lunar surface and is reflected back. The
experiment is deemed a success and a milestone in laser technology.

MAY 10

Film studio magnate Samuel Goldwyn presents the Samuel Goldwyn Screenwriting
Award to a 23-year-old aspiring filmmaker named Francis Ford Coppola.

MAY 11

The United States deploys troops to Thailand.

MAY 12

Light heavyweight boxing champ Archie Moore, who
would retire with a record 131 wins by knockout, surrenders
his title in order to move into the heavyweight class.

MAY 13

Seattle World's Fair general manager Ewan Dingwall shuts down the "Girls of
the Galaxy" exhibit, which features women in "space-age" costumes posing for
pin-up photos, on the grounds that the show violates the fair's decency standards.

MAY 14

Inventor Adolph E. Goldfarb applies for a patent for an animated toothbrush holder, a cartoon rabbit that brushes its teeth along with a child when the toothbrush is removed from the holder. The patent is granted in 1965.

MAY 15

The first American troops are deployed in Laos.

MAY 16

The 100,000th MGA, the most popular British sports car in production and predecessor to the famed MGB, rolls off the assembly line.

MAY 17

President Kennedy is questioned by the press about American troop deployment in Southeast Asia. He replies that troops are only there in a defensive capacity.

MAY 18

The convictions of folk singer Pete Seeger on ten counts of contempt of Congress, for refusing to answer questions from the House Un-American Activities Committee in 1956, are overturned on appeal.

MAY 19

Marilyn Monroe appears at President John F. Kennedy's
birthday party to sing her now-famous rendition of
"Happy Birthday to You." It is her last public performance.

MAY 20

Mr. Acker Bilk, a jazz clarinetist, becomes the first British performer to reach
number one on the U.S. pop charts with his hit "Strangers on the Shore."

MAY 21

George Jones has a number one country hit with "She Thinks I Still Care."

MAY 22

A bomb explodes aboard a Continental Airlines flight over
Unionville, Missouri, killing all 45 passengers and crew.

MAY 23

The Walt Disney film *Bon Voyage!,* starring Jane Wyman and
Fred MacMurray, is the number one movie in the country.

MAY 24

Astronaut Scott Carpenter becomes the second American to orbit the Earth, which he does three times in the *Aurora 7* capsule.

President Kennedy inspects the tiny interior of the *Friendship 7* capsule with astronaut John Glenn.

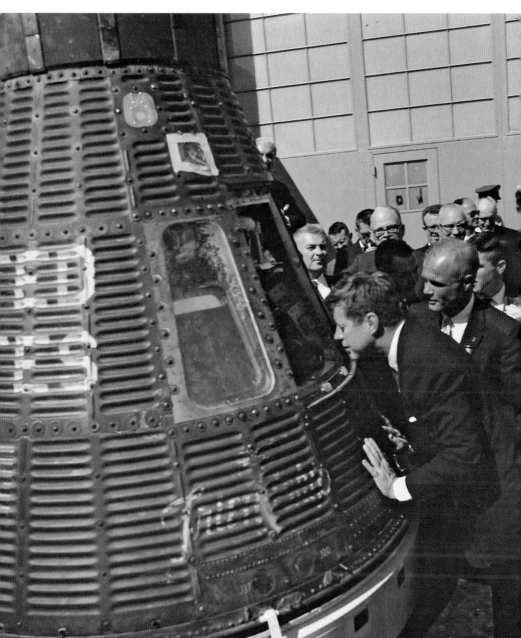

MAY 25

Time magazine reports that the reason William Faulkner, lecturing in Virginia, refuses to attend a White House dinner for Nobel laureates is that "it's 100 miles away. That's a long way to go just to eat."

MAY 26

Detroit Tigers right-fielder Al Kaline sacrifices his right clavicle— and the best season of his career—with a game-saving catch of a New York Yankees fly ball in the bottom of the ninth inning.

MAY 27

Ray Charles's "I Can't Stop Loving You" is the number one single in the country.

MAY 28

Lonely Are the Brave, a Western starring Kirk Douglas, is the top-grossing film in America.

MAY 29

The stock market takes a sudden decline, called a "flash crash," ending the day down 34.95 points, at the time the second-worst one-day drop in stock-market history.

MAY 30

Composer Benjamin Britten's *War Requiem* premieres
at the reconsecration of England's Coventry Cathedral,
a 14th-century landmark destroyed during World War II.

MAY 31

The Israeli government executes Adolf Eichmann, the German SS
officer who presided over the extermination of millions of Jews during
World War II and then fled to Argentina, for crimes against humanity.

JUNE 1

An Air France charter flight carrying civic leaders from
Atlanta, Georgia, overruns the runway at Orly International
Airport, killing 130 passengers and most of the crew.

JUNE 2

Author Vita Sackville-West, known for her novels, her bohemian lifestyle,
and her love affair with fellow author Virginia Woolf, dies at age 70.

JUNE 3

Stanley Kubrick's film version of Vladimir Nabokov's
controversial novel *Lolita* premieres in New York.

JUNE 4

The Beatles sign a recording contract with the EMI record label.

JUNE 5

French architect Jacques Greber dies at age 79. He was the master architect for the 1937 Paris International Exposition and a master planner of the Benjamin Franlin Parkway in Philadelphia, Pennsylvania.

JUNE 6

William Faulkner, the Nobel Prize–winning author of *The Sound and the Fury* and many other classics of Southern literature, dies in Byhalia, Mississippi.

JUNE 7

President Kennedy holds a press conference where he calls for tax cuts, answers questions about foreign policy, and discusses the Surgeon General's plan to investigate links between cigarette smoking and disease.

JUNE 8

Comedian Bob Hope receives the U.S. Congressional Gold Medal, one of the highest civilian honors awarded by the nation.

JUNE 9

Jaipur, an American Thoroughbred, wins the Belmont Stakes.

John Francis Bongiovi Jr. is born on March 2 in Perth Amboy, New Jersey. His future rock-and-roll moniker will be Jon Bon Jovi.

JUNE 10

Major League Baseball teams combined to
hit a one-day record total of 54 home runs.

JUNE 11

Inmates John Anglin, Clarence Anglin, and Frank Lee Morris disappear
from their cells in Alcatraz Prison. Though it is assumed they drowned in
San Francisco Bay, to this day it is believed by many that the men pulled
off the only successful escape from the island prison known as "the Rock."

JUNE 12

17-year-old George Lucas is involved in a horrific car crash
that totals his beloved Fiat Bianchina. The accident will inspire
the final scene in Lucas's film *American Graffiti,* set in 1962.

JUNE 13

U.S. diplomats work to dissuade India from buying
military hardware from the Soviet Union.

JUNE 14

Police discover the body of Anna Slesers, the first of several
victims of Albert DeSalvo, the so-called Boston Strangler.

JUNE 15

The Students for a Democratic Society (SDS) organization completes the Port Huron Statement, a manifesto of its aims and goals, including racial equality and nuclear disarmament. The SDS will be one of the groups at the center of student activism and agitation during the late 1960s.

JUNE 16

Two U.S. Army officers are killed in Saigon, Vietnam.

JUNE 17

Jack Nicklaus wins the U.S Open Championship golf tournament, narrowly edging out Arnold Palmer. Astonishingly, the championship is Nicklaus's first professional win.

JUNE 18

The number one film in America is *That Touch of Mink.*

JUNE 19

The White House issues a national security memorandum that outlines plans to assign U.S. Army Special Forces units to support Central Intelligence Agency operations in Vietnam.

JUNE 20

Jazz saxophonist John Coltrane records his influential album *Impressions.*

JUNE 21

President Kennedy invokes executive powers to delay
a proposed union strike against American Airlines.

JUNE 22

A similar strike proposal against Trans World Airlines is averted as
an accord is reached, calling for a gradual reduction of flight
crew rendered superfluous by advancements in airliner technology.

JUNE 23

The New York Yankees and the Detroit Tigers play the longest game in
baseball history, with the Yankees winning 9–7 in the 22nd inning.

JUNE 24

Boys' Night Out, a comedy starring James Garner, Kim Novak, and
Tony Randall, becomes the top-grossing film in the country.

JUNE 25

The Peace Corps sends its 1,000th volunteer overseas.

At the Century 21 Exposition in Seattle, a woman demonstrates a state-of-the-art kitchen.

JUNE 26

The United States Supreme Court rules mandatory
prayer in public schools unconstitutional.

JUNE 27

Gordon Stanley "Mickey" Cochrane, Hall of Fame
catcher, dies. Mickey Mantle was named for him.

JUNE 28

Several different sects of the Lutheran Church merge
to form the Lutheran Church in America.

JUNE 29

Sir Winston Churchill falls in a Monte Carlo hotel room, breaking his left thigh.

JUNE 30

Brooklyn Dodgers hurler Sandy Koufax pitches his first no-hitter, against the
New York Mets. This marks the beginning of a remarkable five-year stretch
that will distinguish him as one of the greatest pitchers in baseball history.

JULY 1

"The Stripper" by David Rose is the number one pop song in America. Intended as a throwaway B-side and a joke, the tune becomes one of the most recognizable pieces of music ever recorded.

JULY 2

The first Wal-Mart store opens in Rogers, Arkansas.

JULY 3

Claude King's "Wolverton Mountain" is the number one country single on the charts.

JULY 4

The Steve McQueen war movie *Hell Is for Heroes* is the number one movie in America.

JULY 5

Algeria becomes an independent nation.

JULY 6

President Kennedy calls for increased safety measures
to prevent accidental firing of nuclear weapons.

JULY 7

A probe discovers oil fields beneath the basin of the Gulf of Mexico.

JULY 8

Georges Bataille, novelist, philosopher, and leading figure of
what would become known as postmodernism, dies at age 64.

JULY 9

Andy Warhol's *Campbell's Soup Cans* series shows in Los Angeles.

JULY 10

The first telecommunications satellite, Telstar, is launched into orbit.

JULY 11

Bobby Vinton's "Roses Are Red (My Love)" tops the American pop charts.

Dodger Stadium, located in an area formerly known as Chevez Ravine, opens on April 10.

JULY 12

The Rolling Stones make their debut at the Marquee Club, London.

JULY 13

Arnold Palmer wins the Open Championship (known outside the United Kingdom as "the British Open") at the Royal Troon Club, Scotland.

JULY 14

Baseball legend Hank Aaron hits his 500th career home run.

JULY 15

The Music Man, an adaptation of a 1957 Broadway musical, is the top-grossing film in the country.

JULY 16

A U.S. Army helicopter is shot down by insurgents in Vietnam.

JULY 17

Soviet Premier Khrushchev announces that the USSR possesses an anti-missile missile system and derides the U.S. for its high-altitude nuclear testing.

JULY 18

A Soviet fighter jet makes a few close passes at an American passenger jet over Berlin.

JULY 19

President Kennedy announces that he has appointed a dozen men and women to a Consumers' Advisory Council, which will serve as a voice for American consumers to the White House.

JULY 20

Great Britain introduces the world's first passenger hovercraft service, ferrying between England and Wales.

JULY 21

President Kennedy reassigns key members of his top military staff, including the chairman of the Joint Chiefs of Staff and the commander of U.S. and NATO forces in Europe.

JULY 22

South African golfer Gary Player wins the PGA
Championship in Newtown Square, Pennsylvania.

JULY 23

Telstar relays the first live trans-Atlantic television signal.

JULY 24

Eastern airlines rejects efforts by labor secretary Arthur J. Goldberg to
arbitrate the flight engineers' strike that has grounded the airline.

JULY 25

The U.S. Army forms the first combat helicopter unit,
deploying the UH-1 ("Huey") for formation attacks.

JULY 26

The House of Representatives approves a bill calling
for an end to wage discrimination against women.

JULY 27

President Kennedy signs sweeping welfare-reform legislation into law.

William Faulkner, one of the greatest American novelists of all time, dies in Byhalia, Mississippi, on June 6.

JULY 28

Martin Luther King Jr. and 27 others are arrested in Albany, Georgia, while holding a "prayer protest" against racial inequality.

JULY 29

A passenger train derails outside Harrisburg, Pennsylvania, killing 22.

JULY 30

Project Apollo, whose aim is sending three astronauts to the moon, is announced by NASA.

JULY 31

An annular solar eclipse occurs in the Northern Hemisphere.

AUGUST 1

President Kennedy pledges over $200 million for Project Gemini, a series of two-man orbital space missions to train astronauts for deep-space work.

AUGUST 2

The White House urges officials in Albany, Georgia, to meet with black citizens to work out racial tensions in the city.

AUGUST 3

Dean Cromwell, track and football coach at the University of Southern California, dies at age 82. Cromwell was known as the "Maker of Champions" for the many Olympic gold medalists he trained.

AUGUST 4

Australian advisers arrive in South Vietnam to instruct anti-insurgent forces in jungle warfare.

AUGUST 5

Marilyn Monroe is discovered dead from an overdose of barbituates. It is undetermined whether or not she committed suicide.

AUGUST 6

Jamaica becomes an independent nation.

AUGUST 7

Legendary country singer Patsy Cline releases
Sentimentally Yours, which would be her final album.

AUGUST 8

Neil Sedaka has a number one hit with "Breaking Up Is Hard to Do."

AUGUST 9

Nobel Laureate Herman Hesse, author of
Siddhartha and *Steppenwolf,* dies in Switzerland.

AUGUST 10

The first appearance of Marvel Comics' iconic superhero Spider-Man, created
by Stan Lee and Steve Ditko, occurs in *Amazing Fantasy* number 15.

AUGUST 11

Soviet spaceship *Vostok 3,* with cosmonaut
Andriyan Nikolayev on board, is launched.

AUGUST 12

The Soviets launch cosmonaut Pavel Popvich in *Vostok 4*, the first time more than one manned spacecraft at a time has been deployed. The two capsules pass within four miles of each other.

The boy who would become Tom Cruise is born Thomas Cruise Mapother IV on July 3 in Syracuse, New York.

AUGUST 13

Mabel Dodge Luhan, patron of many important artists such as Ansel Adams, Georgia O'Keeffe, and Willa Cather, dies at age 83.

AUGUST 14

The number one movie in America is *Kid Galahad,* starring Elvis Presley.

AUGUST 15

Soviet space capsule *Vostok 3* lands after making a record 64 orbits around Earth.

AUGUST 16

Ringo Starr (born Richard Starkey) replaces Pete Best as drummer for the Beatles.

AUGUST 17

General Douglas MacArthur, 82, is honored by Congress for more than 50 years of military service and command.

AUGUST 18

"If I Had a Hammer," the first of many hits for folk trio Peter, Paul & Mary, is released.

AUGUST 19

Little Eva, formerly songwriter Carole King's babysitter, has a number one pop hit with "The Loco-Motion."

AUGUST 20

Dr, James Van Allen, discoverer of the Van Allen radiation belt, announces that high-altitude nuclear testing above the Pacific has created a new belt.

AUGUST 21

U.S. officials ascertain that 15 Soviet ships that are docked in Cuba do not carry Communist troops, as Cuban refugees have claimed.

AUGUST 22

The world's first nuclear-powered ship, the USS *Savannah,* completes its first voyage, from Yorktown, Pennsylvania, to Savannah, Georgia.

AUGUST 29

The federal government opens a lawsuit to strike down what it perceives as Mississippi's prohibitive eligibility regulations designed to keep African Americans from voting.

AUGUST 30

U.S. Supreme Court Justice Felix Frankfurter retires.

AUGUST 31

The islands of Trinidad and Tobago together become an independent nation, the Republic of Trinidad and Tobago.

SEPTEMBER 1

The United Nations announces that Earth's population has reached three billion.

SEPTEMBER 2

The Soviet Union agrees to an arms pact with Cuba.

SEPTEMBER 3

Beloved and influential poet E.E. Cummings dies at age 67 in New Hampshire.

SEPTEMBER 4

"Devil Woman" is a number one country hit for Marty Robbins.

SEPTEMBER 5

The Music Man climbs back to the top of the pile to hold the number one film spot for another four weeks.

SEPTEMBER 6

Unknown assailants fire shotguns into a house in Dawson, Georgia, where voter-registration workers are staying.

SEPTEMBER 7

Karen Blixen, the Danish author of *Out of Africa* (under the pen name Isak Dinesen), dies at age 77.

SEPTEMBER 8

The first Soviet missiles arrive in Cuba.

SEPTEMBER 9

The Four Seasons' "Sherry" becomes their first number one hit song.

SEPTEMBER 10

Two black churches near Sasser, Georgia, are destroyed by arson. FBI agents investigating the scenes are physically attacked.

SEPTEMBER 11

The Soviet Union declares that an American attack on Cuba or on Soviet shipments to the island will be considered an act of war.

SEPTEMBER 12

During an address at Rice University in Houston, President Kennedy reaffirms his pledge that NASA will put a man on the moon by the end of the decade.

SEPTEMBER 13

"Ramblin' Rose" by Nat King Cole tops the easy-listening charts.

On August 5, actress Marilyn Monroe—shown here performing with the USO in South Korea—is found dead of a drug overdose in her home in Los Angeles.

SEPTEMBER 14

President Kennedy admonishes Americans for "loose talk"
suggesting that the U.S. plans to invade Cuba.

SEPTEMBER 15

A piece of space debris discovered in Wisconsin is determined to be from the
Soviet satellite *Sputnik 4,* prompting debate over the enactment of space laws.

SEPTEMBER 16

Iran announces that it will allow no foreign military installations within
its borders. Soviet officials call on other nations to do the same.

SEPTEMBER 17

Thousands of American military personnel are deployed to South Vietnam
to train and advise in the fight against Communist insurgents.

SEPTEMBER 18

U.S. Marines conduct the first American combat
operation from Da Nang, in Vietnam.

SEPTEMBER 19

Running in the special election to fill his brother's seat
in the U.S. Senate, Edward M. Kennedy easily defeats
his opponent in the Massachusetts Democratic primary.

SEPTEMBER 20

Congress votes on a joint resolution approving force to counter Cuban
aggression against other states in the Western Hemisphere.

SEPTEMBER 21

China and India engage in a border conflict, creating unrest
in southern Asia that will become the Sino-Indian War.

SEPTEMBER 22

A federal district judge dismisses contempt charges against three
University of Mississippi officials seeking to block integration
of the college. A few days later the University will give in to
federal pressures and admit a black student seeking to enroll.

SEPTEMBER 23

The Jetsons, an animated family sitcom set in the future, premieres on
ABC, becoming the first program on that network to air in color.

SEPTEMBER 24

Philharmonic Hall, the first part of what will be the Lincoln Center for the Arts, opens in New York City.

SEPTEMBER 25

Sonny Liston makes boxing history by being the first fighter ever to knock out a reigning heavyweight champ in the first round, taking Floyd Patterson's title in Chicago.

SEPTEMBER 26

The Beverly Hillbillies debuts on CBS.

SEPTEMBER 27

Silent Spring, by Rachel Carson, widely considered the beginning of the modern environmentalist movement, is published.

SEPTEMBER 28

President Kennedy opens a White House summit on drug abuse, with the goal of establishing a federal narcotics program.

SEPTEMBER 29

Canada launches its first satellite, *Alouette 1,* into space.

SEPTEMBER 30

Cesar Chavez forms the United Farm Workers organization.

In 1962, with funds borrowed from the Teamsters Central States Pension Fund, cabana motel owner Jay Sarno began building a 14-story casino he would name Caesars Palace.

OCTOBER 1

James Meredith, the first black student at the newly desegregated University of Mississippi, is escorted past a violent mob of protesters to enroll.

OCTOBER 2

Heinrich Deubel, commandant of the Nazi concentration camp Dachau, dies at age 72.

OCTOBER 3

The horror film *Carnival of Souls* is the number one movie in America.

OCTOBER 4

Commander Walter Schirra completes six Earth orbits, twice as many as the previous two manned spaceflights.

OCTOBER 5

The Beatles release their first single, "Love Me Do."

OCTOBER 6

Tod Browning, director of the film classics *Dracula* (starring Bela Lugosi) and *Freaks,* dies in Malibu, California at age 82.

OCTOBER 7

Cuban President Osvaldo Dorticos warns the United Nations General Assembly that Cuba is prepared to defend itself against invasion.

OCTOBER 8

The Longest Day is the top-grossing film in the country.

OCTOBER 9

Uganda becomes an independent nation.

OCTOBER 10

Secretary of state Dean Rusk pledges economic aid to Cuba if it abolishes Communist rule.

OCTOBER 11

The Second Vatican Council, popularly known as "Vatican II,"
opens. The decisions reached at these meetings will
have far-reaching effects on the Catholic church worldwide.

OCTOBER 12

Typhoon Freda, a category 5 event dubbed the "Columbus Day
Storm," strikes the Pacific Northwest and western Canada,
killing 46 and doing a quarter of a billion dollars' worth of damage.

OCTOBER 13

Edward Albee's classic play *Who's Afraid
of Virginia Woolf?* makes its Broadway debut.

OCTOBER 14

An American U-2 spy plane gathers photographs
of new military construction in Cuba.

OCTOBER 15

The Central Intelligence Agency determines that the Soviets have
installed medium-range ballistic missiles in Cuba. National security adviser
McGeorge Bundy and defense secretary Robert McNamara are notified. President
Kennedy is briefed the next morning, thus beginning the Cuban Missile Crisis.

OCTOBER 16

The New York Yankees defeat the San Francisco Giants in the seventh game of the World Series in San Francisco. Several games are postponed due to rain, stretching the series to 13 days, the longest Fall Classic played to date.

OCTOBER 17

Soviet premier Khrushchev sends a personal message to President Kennedy denying the existence of Soviet missiles in Cuba.

The 1962 Lana Lobell catalog shows ladies "the way to look." At bottom right, "An evening gem in a dazzle of rayon chiffon brings out your inner fascination!"

OCTOBER 18

Soviet Minister of Foreign Affairs Andrei Gromyko tells President Kennedy that any weapons in Cuba are purely defensive.

OCTOBER 19

U-2 reconnaissance reveals four operational missile sites in Cuba. The U.S. military begins to mobilize for immediate action, including a possible invasion of Cuba.

OCTOBER 20

"Monster Mash" by Bobby "Boris" Picket and the Crypt-Kickers begins its second week atop the American pop charts.

OCTOBER 21

President Kennedy meets with his top military and intelligence advisers to decide between strategic air strikes against Cuban military targets and a naval blockade against Soviet ships en route to the island.

OCTOBER 22

President Kennedy gives a nationally televised address announcing the presence of Soviet missiles in Cuba, a planned American naval blockade, and his willingness to use nuclear retaliation against the Soviets should hostilities commence. At the same time, the American military is ordered to go to DEFCON 3, meaning heightened preparation for an increased threat of nuclear war.

OCTOBER 23

Talks begin with Turkey and NATO to withdraw U.S. missile installations from Turkey as a negotiating point with the Soviets to defuse the Cuban Missile Crisis.

OCTOBER 24

Premier Khrushchev denounces the American blockade of Soviet transport ships to Cuba as a "pirate action" that will lead to war.

OCTOBER 25

John Steinbeck, author of *The Grapes of Wrath* and other works, receives the Nobel Prize in Literature "for his realistic and imaginative writings, combining as they do sympathetic humour and keen social perception."

OCTOBER 26

The U.S. military is ordered to go to DEFCON 2, with American bombers made ready to take off on 15 minutes' notice.

OCTOBER 27

A U.S. Air Force spy plane is shot down over Cuban airspace, prompting the military to urge President Kennedy to order an immediate invasion of Cuba. Meanwhile, Premier Khrushchev proposes that U.S. missiles be removed from Turkey and Italy in exchange for the removal of Soviet missiles from Cuba.

OCTOBER 28

A pact is reached between President Kennedy and Premier Khrushchev calling for the removal of missiles from Cuba and Turkey, and for the acknowledgement of Cuban sovereignty. The Cuban Missile Crisis ends. It is the closest the world has ever come to nuclear war.

OCTOBER 29

"He's a Rebel" by the Crystals is the number one pop single in America.

OCTOBER 30

Bill Anderson's "Mama Sang a Song" tops the country charts.

OCTOBER 31

The number one easy-listening single is
"Only Love Can Break a Heart" by Gene Pitney.

NOVEMBER 1

The Soviet Union begins to take down its missile installations in Cuba.

NOVEMBER 2

Godfrey Lowell Cabot, millionaire philanthropist and aviator known
for his endowments for MIT and his work in suppressing "offensive" books
by authors like William Faulkner and Ernest Hemingway, dies at age 101.

NOVEMBER 3

The United States and the Soviet Union agree to allow the International
Red Cross to monitor the dismantling of weapons structures in Cuba.

For 13 long days in October, the United States and the Soviet Union face off in what will
come to be known as the Cuban Missile Crisis. Pictured is an aerial photo of the San
Cristobal missile launch site in Cuba.

MRBM LAUNCH SITE 2
SAN CRISTOBAL
1 NOVEMBER 1962

FUEL TRAILERS

MISSILE-READY TENT

FORMER LAUNCH POSITIONS

FORMER LOCATION OF MISSILE-READY TENTS

NOVEMBER 4

Enos, the first chimpanzee to orbit the Earth, dies. NASA determines that his death is unrelated to his career as an astronaut.

NOVEMBER 5

The number one film in America is *What Ever Happened to Baby Jane?,* starring Joan Crawford and Bette Davis.

NOVEMBER 6

The United Nations General Assembly issues a blanket condemnation of South Africa's policy of apartheid and calls for all nations to sever ties with that country.

NOVEMBER 7

Former First Lady Eleanor Roosevelt, an activist and ambassador in her own right, dies at age 78.

NOVEMBER 8

Richard M. Nixon utters his now-famous words "You won't have Dick Nixon to kick around any more" after losing the race for governor of California, two years after losing the presidential race to John F. Kennedy.

NOVEMBER 9

President Kennedy orders all American flags to be
flown at half-staff in honor of Eleanor Roosevelt.

NOVEMBER 10

"I've Been Everywhere" is a chart-topping country hit for Hank Snow.

NOVEMBER 11

The Four Seasons have their second number one single with "Big Girls Don't Cry."

NOVEMBER 12

The remake of *Mutiny on the Bounty*, starring
Marlon Brando, is number one at the box office.

NOVEMBER 13

"All Alone Am I" by Brenda Lee is the
number one easy-listening hit in America.

NOVEMBER 14

President Kennedy and Soviet ambassador Dobrynin
attend a performance of the Bolshoi Ballet, the president's
first public appearance since the start of the Cuban Missile Crisis.

NOVEMBER 15

It is revealed that both President Kennedy and his brother, attorney
general Robert Kennedy, donate their salaries to charity, something
the elder Kennedy has done since he became a congressman in 1947.

NOVEMBER 16

Fidel Castro issues a threat to the United Nations that he will order
American reconnaissance planes over Cuban airspace shot down.

NOVEMBER 17

President Kennedy dedicates Dulles International Airport,
named after former secretary of state John Foster Dulles,
to serve as a municipal airport for the Washington, D.C., area.

NOVEMBER 18

Niels Bohr, the Nobel Prize–winning physicist who made
vital discoveries in atomic structure and participated in
the Manhattan Project (the atomic bomb), dies at age 77.

NOVEMBER 19

The Evpatoria Planetary Radar in Russia beams a message in Morse code to the planet Venus. The message reads "MIR, LENIN, SSSR." Translation from Russian: "peace, Lenin, CCCP" (the Russian acronym for "USSR").

NOVEMBER 20

President Kennedy signs Executive Order 11063, prohibiting discrimination in housing because of race. This is regarded as a major civil-rights victory.

Eight hundred women hold a strike for peace near the United Nations building during the Cuban Missile Crisis.

NOVEMBER 21

What Ever Happened to Baby Jane? returns to number one.

NOVEMBER 22

China announces a cease-fire in the Sino-Indian War.

NOVEMBER 23

The Atomic Energy Commission reports that nuclear power plants are on the verge of going online, predicting that by the year 2000 such plants will provide the majority of the nation's electricity.

NOVEMBER 24

India meets with American and British officials about possible material support should hostilities resume with China.

NOVEMBER 25

The number one movie in America is now
Girls! Girls! Girls!, starring Elvis Presley.

NOVEMBER 26

The Beatles record "Please Please Me" in London.

NOVEMBER 27

It is announced that disarmament talks between the United States and the Soviet Union have yielded no results.

NOVEMBER 28

Queen Wilhelmina of the Netherlands dies at age 82.

NOVEMBER 29

Great Britain and France agree to begin joint construction on the Concorde supersonic passenger jet.

NOVEMBER 30

U Thant of Burma becomes secretary-general of the United Nations.

DECEMBER 1

The Kennedy administration steps up its proposed
timetable for a moon landing, from 1968 to mid-1967.

DECEMBER 2

Senate majority leader Mike Mansfield becomes the first U.S. official to
express public concern over the conduct of military operations in Vietnam.

DECEMBER 3

The Peace Corps announces a shift in its focus, toward aid in Latin America.

DECEMBER 4

The White House confirms that Soviet bombers are being shipped out of
Cuba in compliance with the accord that ended the Cuban Missile Crisis.

DECEMBER 5

Comedian Lenny Bruce is arrested on obscenity charges in Chicago, Illinois,
the second time this year he has been arrested over his controversial act.

DECEMBER 6

Bob Dylan begins recording his second album in New York.

DECEMBER 7

Bassist Bill Wyman joins the Rolling Stones.

Two South Vietnamese Air Force T-28C Trojan aircraft scour the Vietnamese coastline during a counterinsurgency training mission.

DECEMBER 8

The New York City newspaper strike begins when union workers walk off the job at New York's nine major newspapers. The strike would last until March 1963 and raise the profile of news radio, magazines, and other alternative media as newspapers are forced to cut circulation.

DECEMBER 9

President Kennedy questions scientists at Project Rover in Nevada when a manned mission to Mars might be feasible.

DECEMBER 10

Martin Luther King, visiting South Africa, calls for action against the policy of apartheid in that country.

DECEMBER 11

James Watson, Nobel Laureate in Medicine for his work on the structure of DNA, delivers his lecture "The Involvement of RNA in the Synthesis of Proteins."

DECEMBER 12

The Minuteman Intercontinental Missile is introduced by the United States Air Force. It is announced that 20 of the missiles are installed and operational.

DECEMBER 13

Steve Lawrence has a number one
easy-listening hit with "Go Away Little Girl."

DECEMBER 14

Mariner 2, an American space probe, passes Venus and sends
the first transmission of extraplanetary data ever collected.

DECEMBER 15

Actor and director Charles Laughton, famous for his portrayal
of Captain Bligh in *Mutiny on the Bounty* and for directing
The Night of the Hunter, dies in Hollywood at age 63.

DECEMBER 16

The Tornados' surf-instrumental classic "Telstar" tops the U.S. pop charts.

DECEMBER 17

Lawrence of Arabia, starring Peter O'Toole as T.E. Lawrence, has the
highest-grossing weekend opening of 1962. The film would go on
to win numerous awards and be considered a cinema masterpiece.

DECEMBER 18

President Kennedy gives a televised address to the nation expressing pessimism for American-Soviet relations in the foreseeable future.

DECEMBER 19

An American military team is dispatched to the war-torn Congo to study the civil conflict there.

DECEMBER 20

The *Mona Lisa* goes on display in New York.

DECEMBER 21

Pan American and TWA airlines agree to merge.

DECEMBER 22

The White House approves nearly $6 billion in funding for the space program, 75% of which is earmarked for moonshot operations.

DECEMBER 23

The Dallas Texans defeat the Houston Oilers 20–17 in double overtime to win the American Football League playoffs in Houston.

DECEMBER 24

Cuba exchanges the last 1,113 prisoners of the 1961 Bay of Pigs invasion to the United States for $53 million worth of foodstuffs.

A billboard illustrates John Steinbeck's novel *The Grapes of Wrath* along a California highway. Steinbeck receives the Nobel Prize in Literature on October 25.

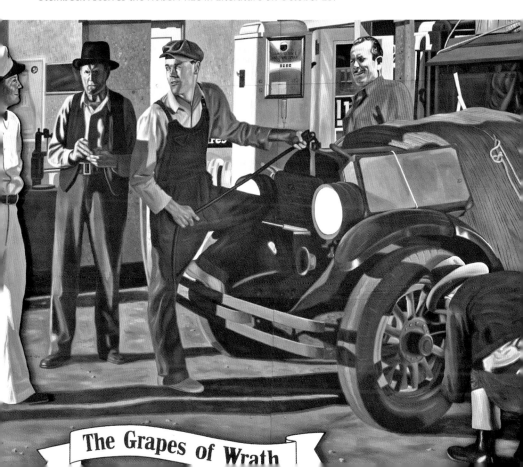

DECEMBER 25

Walt Disney Productions' *In Search of the Castaways*
knocks *Lawrence of Arabia* out of first place.

DECEMBER 26

The Bay of Pigs prisoners, along with about 1,000 relatives also
released from Cuba, reunite with their families in Miami, Florida.

DECEMBER 27

The Soviet Union conducts several nuclear weapons tests before
a new moratorium is scheduled to begin on January 1, 1963.

DECEMBER 28

President Kennedy meets with the Bay of Pigs prisoners in Palm Beach, Florida.

DECEMBER 29

"Don't Let Me Cross Over" by Carl Butler and Pearl
is the number one country single in America.

DECEMBER 30

The Green Bay Packers win the National Football League playoffs, beating the New York Giants 16–7 at Yankee Stadium.

DECEMBER 31

Lawrence of Arabia is once again the top-grossing film in America.

Former First Lady Eleanor Roosevelt, seen here in New York City, passes away on November 7 in her home in Manhattan.

Barbra Streisand, at age 19, is on the fast track to stardom, appearing on Broadway as Miss Marmelstein in the 1962 musical *I Can Get It for You Wholesale*.

Pop Culture in
1962

Though most of us regard history as a panorama of important battles, elections, legislation, and speeches by world leaders and generals and statesmen, it is also of historical significance to look at our entertainments and pastimes. These things help to form the history of the people. They tell us what captured our attention, excited our imagination, and helped us get through turbulent times.

The list of most popular and well-received films, TV shows, music, and theater, paints an interesting picture. Although the presence of television in most American households had hurt the movie industry, audiences still flocked to light comedies and human dramas as well as epic action flicks. On TV, we preferred lightweight distraction in half-hour doses—of the top 10 shows, 7 were sitcoms, two were Westerns, and only one was a straight-up drama. Rock and roll singles dominated the charts, on its way to becoming the standard for pop music and edging easy-listening and orchestral music onto niche radio and album-only formats.

In 1962 we wanted to laugh and dance as the world got more complicated around us.

The Beatles are on the verge of superstardom. Everything any one of them touches for the next decade would become more valuable just for having been handled by a Beatle—like this guitar, shared by John Lennon, Paul McCartney, and George Harrison while playing in Germany in 1962.

The 10 best-reviewed films:
> *To Kill a Mockingbird*
> *Lawrence of Arabia*
> *Lolita*
> *Dr. No*
> *The Longest Day*
> *The Manchurian Candidate*
> *The Man Who Shot Liberty Valance*
> *The Miracle Worker*
> *Harakiri*
> *The Exterminating Angel*

Ian Fleming's James Bond books were a relatively minor phenomenon in publishing until, in an interview, President Kennedy casually mentioned that he was a fan. Sales of the books immediately shot up and prompted United Artists to film *Dr. No*. Fleming had strong objections to the casting of Sean Connery as Bond (he wanted David Niven), but nobody could argue with the runaway success of the film franchise, now the longest-running film series in history.

The 10 top-grossing films:
> *Lawrence of Arabia,* $20,310,000
> *The Longest Day,* $17,600,000
> *In Search of the Castaways,* $9,975,000
> *What Ever Happened to Baby Jane?,* $9,000,000
> *The Music Man,* $8,100,000
> *Dr. No,* $8,000,000
> *That Touch of Mink,* $7,942,000
> *Mutiny on the Bounty,* $7,410,000
> *To Kill a Mockingbird,* $7,112,000
> *Gypsy,* $6,350,000

Academy Awards:
> Best Picture: *Lawrence of Arabia,* Horizon-Spiegel-Lean, Columbia
> Best Director: David Lean, *Lawrence of Arabia*
> Best Actor: Gregory Peck, *To Kill a Mockingbird*
> Best Actress: Anne Bancroft, *The Miracle Worker*
> Best Supporting Actor: Ed Begley, *Sweet Bird of Youth*
> Best Supporting Actress: Patty Duke, *The Miracle Worker*
> Best Foreign Language Film: *Sundays and Cybele (Les dimanches de ville d'Avray)*

4000 pounds of fireworks

Every day is the Fourth of July with Thunderbird's Sports Roadster—for what other car packs such zip and sparkle, such. Roman candle response into a sleek torpedo shape? What other car looks like action even when it's parked (or conceals its four-seater practicality under the slip-stream headrests of a lift-off tonneau cover)? Best of all, this fire and flair is matched by a marvelous elegance of craftsmanship, a road-leveling solidity that makes cruising seem like coasting. What does 4000 pounds of fireworks feel like? Let your Ford Dealer show you a car as gay as the glitter of its wire-spoked wheels.

Thunderbird
Sports Roadster

The 10 highest-rated U.S. television shows:

> *The Beverly Hillbillies* (CBS)
> *Candid Camera* (CBS)
> *The Red Skelton Show* (CBS)
> *Bonanza* (NBC)
> *The Lucy Show* (CBS)
> *The Andy Griffith Show* (CBS)
> *Ben Casey* (ABC)
> *The Danny Thomas Show* (CBS)
> *The Dick Van Dyke Show* (CBS)
> *Gunsmoke* (CBS)

The Lucy Show almost didn't get made, as Lucille Ball and her *I Love Lucy* costar Desi Arnaz had divorced, and the network was unsure of Ball's ability to carry a show by herself. The ratings, obviously, proved them wrong.

Primetime Emmy Awards:

> Outstanding Drama Series: *The Defenders* (CBS)
> Outstanding Comedy Series: *The Bob Newhart Show* (NBC)
> Outstanding Variety Series: *The Garry Moore Show* (CBS)
> Outstanding Continued Performance by an Actor in a Series:
>   E.G. Marshall, *The Defenders*
> Outstanding Continued Performance by an Actress in a Series:
>   Shirley Booth, *Hazel*
> Outstanding Single Performance by an Actor in a Leading Role:
>   Peter Falk, *The Dick Powell Theatre*, "The Price of Tomatoes"
> Outstanding Single Performance by an Actress in a Leading Role:
>   Julie Harris, *Hallmark Hall of Fame*, "Victoria Regina"

The 10 best-selling albums:

> Leonard Bernstein, *West Side Story* (orchestral score)
> Ray Charles, *Modern Sounds in Country & Western Music*
> Stan Getz & Charlie Byrd, *Jazz Samba*
> Henry Mancini, *Breakfast at Tiffany's* (motion picture soundtrack)
> Vaughn Meader, *The First Family*
> *West Side Story* (cast recording)
> Tony Bennett, *I Left My Heart in San Francisco*
> Allan Sherman, *My Son, the Folk Singer*
> Elvis Presley, *Pot Luck*
> Elvis Presley, *Girls! Girls! Girls!*

Seattle's "Space Needle" is built for the 1962 World's Fair (formally called the Century 21 Exposition). It would become a landmark of the Pacific Northwest.

Although Elvis Presley's work in movies, and subsequent soundtracks, led many in the music industry to write him off as irrelevant, he actually became a bigger star than ever as a result of the two or three films per year he made throughout the decade. In terms of aggregate box-office figures, Elvis Presley was the number one movie star of the 1960s.

The 10 best-selling singles:

Acker Bilk, "Stranger On the Shore"
Ray Charles, "I Can't Stop Loving You"
Dee Dee Sharp, "Mashed Potato Time"
Bobby Vinton, "Roses Are Red (My Love)"
David Rose, "The Stripper"
Shelley Fabares, "Johnny Angel"
Little Eva, "The Loco-Motion"
The Sensations, "Let Me In"
Chubby Checker, "The Twist"
The Shirelles, "Soldier Boy"

Grammy Awards:

Record of the Year: Henry Mancini, "Moon River"
Album of the Year: Judy Garland, *Judy at Carnegie Hall*
Song of the Year: Henry Mancini & Johnny Mercer (songwriters),
    "Moon River"
Best New Artist: Peter Nero
Best Solo Vocal Performance, Female: Judy Garland, *Judy at Carnegie Hall*
Best Solo Vocal Performance, Male: Jack Jones, "Lollipops and Roses"
Best Performance by a Vocal Group: Lambert, Hendricks & Ross, *High Flying*
Best Rock and Roll Recording: Chubby Checker, "Let's Twist Again"
Best Country & Western Recording: Jimmy Dean, "Big Bad John"
Best Rhythm & Blues Recording: Ray Charles, "Hit the Road, Jack"

Tony Awards:

Outstanding Play: *A Man for All Seasons*
Outstanding Musical: *How to Succeed in Business Without Really Trying*
Distinguished Dramatic Actor: Paul Scofield, *A Man for All Seasons*
Distinguished Dramatic Actress: Margaret Leighton, *The Night of the Iguana*
Distinguished Musical Actor: Robert Morse, *How to Succeed in Business
    Without Really Trying*
Distinguished Musical Actress: Anna Maria Alberghetti, *Carnival,* and
    Diahann Carroll, *No Strings* (tie)

Credits and Acknowledgments

John Nettles wrote text and selected images. Individual image credits are as follows.

Chapter 1. Rosie O'Donnell—David Shankbone. Steve Carell—Sergeant Michael Connors, U.S. Army. Demi Moore—David Shankbone. Jon Stewart—Luke Ford.

Chapter 2. Long-distance instructions—Southwestern Bell. House plan—SportSuburban. Gas-station illustration—Texaco advertising image.

Chapter 3. President Kennedy—National Archives. McDonald's arch—Bruce W. Stracener. Fidel Castro at U.N.—Warren K. Leffler. Airplane spraying defoliant—U.S. Air Force. Lucky Luciano mug shot—New York Police Department. Axl Rose—Ed Vill. Jacqueline Kennedy—Mark Shaw. Tetra Pak ad—Tetra Pak. Television showing "Glenn's Voice"—Marion S. Trikosko. President Kennedy inspecting space capsule—NASA. Jon Bon Jovi—Artur Bogdanski. Model kitchen—Seattle Municipal Archives. Dodger Stadium—Rob Reiring. William Faulkner—Carl van Vechten. Tom Cruise—Alan Light. Martin Luther King Jr.—O. Fernandez, *New York World-Telegram & Sun*. Marilyn Monroe—U.S. Army. Caesars Palace—jimg944. Lana Lobell catalog page—SportSuburban. Aerial view, Cuban missiles—National Archives. Women on strike—Phil Stanziola, *New York World-Telegram & Sun*. South Vietnamese pilots in training—U.S. Air Force. *Grapes of Wrath* billboard—Carol M. Highsmith. Eleanor Roosevelt—National Archives.

Chapter 4. Barbra Streisand—*New York World-Telegram & Sun*. Guitar—Magnus Manske. Ford Thunderbird ad—Alden Jewell. Space Needle—Andrew E. Larsen.